MW01488949

Zeke sees a Bug

Written by Kelly Robertson

Illustrated by John Konecny

Kelly Robertson lives with her husband in Thiensville, Wisconsin. She was formerly a kindergarten teacher, but she has been a dental assistant for the past 25-plus years.

In 2002, Kelly rescued Zeke from the Oshkosh Shelter. Zeke was so full of life and love, Kelly always said that Zeke should be "discovered." Kelly recorded their events together, and though *Zeke Sees a Bug* is fiction, the series to follow, *The Adventures of Zeke*, recounts actual events put into story form. Kelly hopes these stories will bring as much joy to her readers as Zeke brought to many people in real life.

This book is dedicated to the memory of my beloved Zeke, to my sister Tracey for her input, to my husband Jim for being my constant "cheering section," and to the Lord for the inspiration of this book.

My Zeke-angel in Lake Michigan
October, 2006.

Published by Orange Hat Publishing 2014

ISBN 978-1-937165-69-7

Copyrighted © 2014, 2015, 2016 by Kelly Robertson
All Rights Reserved
Second Edition

Printed in the United States of America

www.orangehatpublishing.com

Zeke is resting on the bed.

A bug has landed on the window.

The bug plods up the window:
Plink . . . ,
plink,
plink

The bug plods down the window.
Plonk,
plonk,
plonk . . .

The bug sees Zeke.

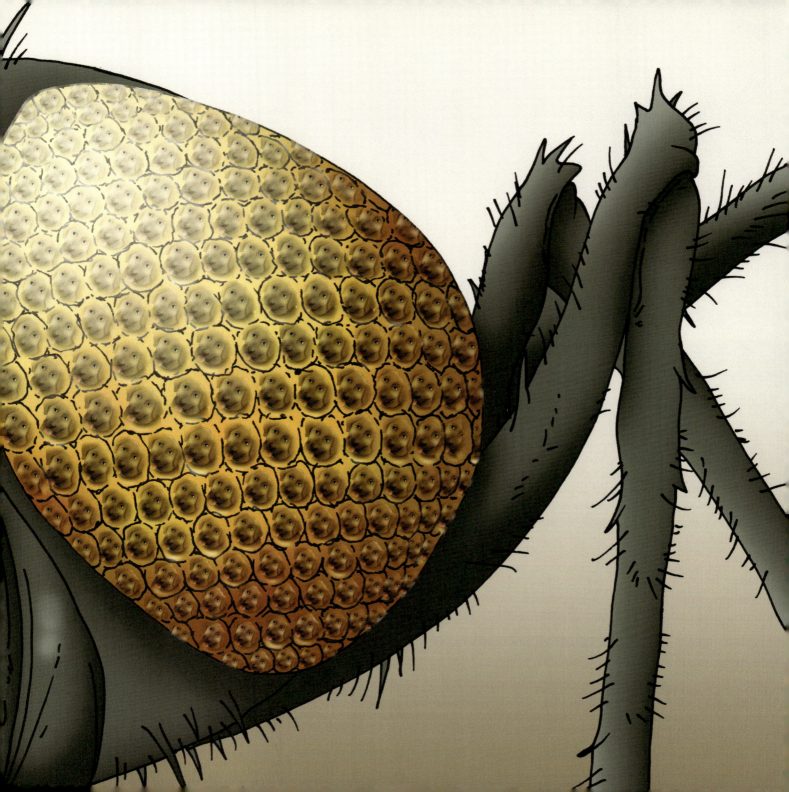

Flyby . . .

Circle about . . .

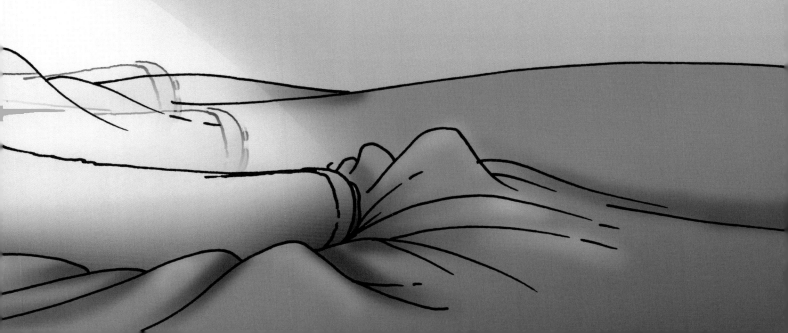

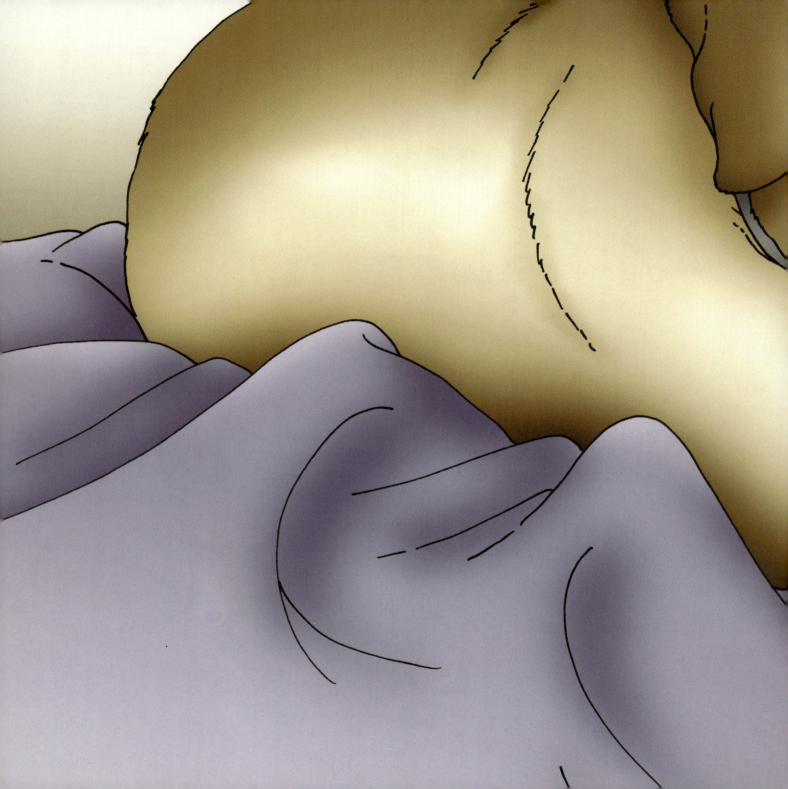

The bug flies away.

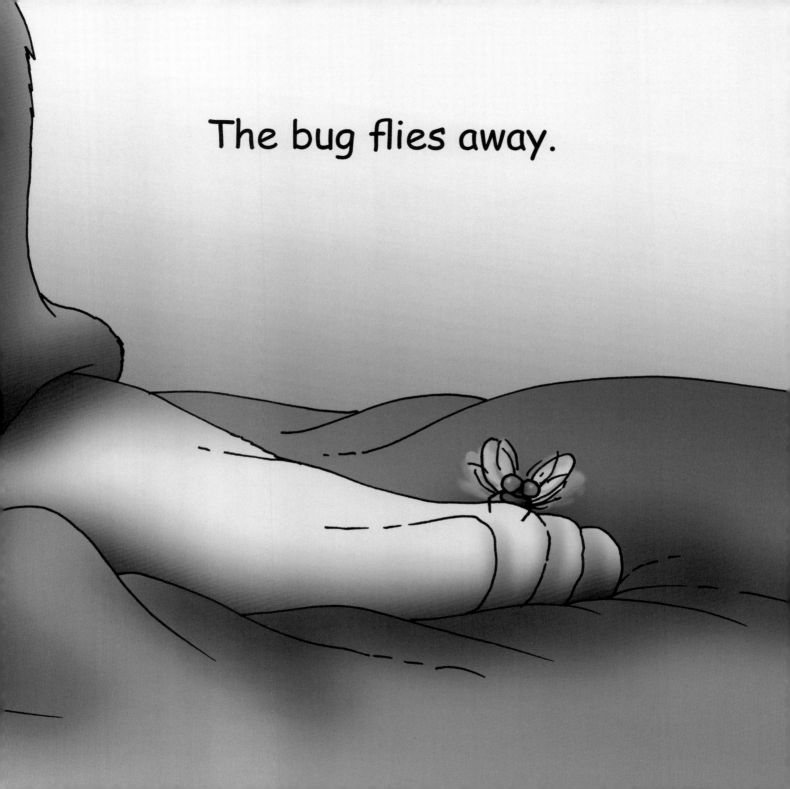

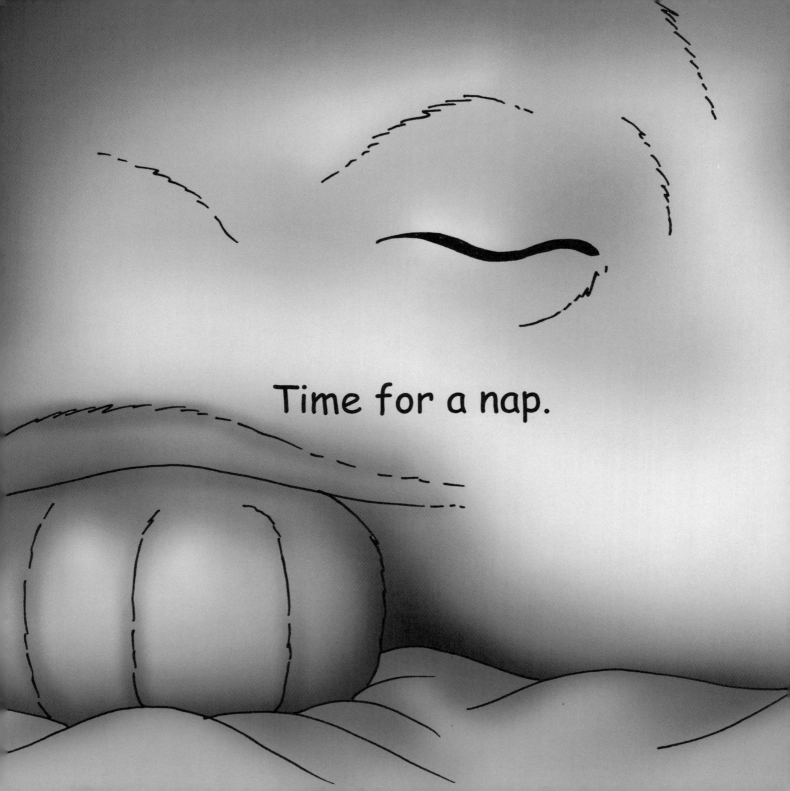

Time for a nap.

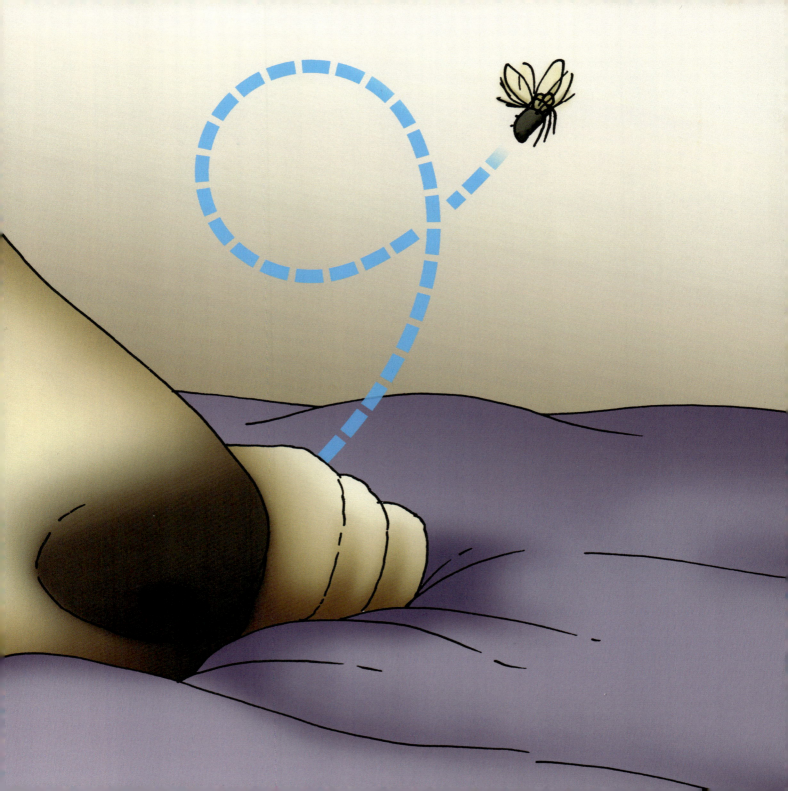

CPSIA information can be obtained at www.ICGtesting.com
Printed in the USA
LVIW01n1551150716
496471LV00002B/2